T0277422

MIDWOOD

MIDWOOD

poems

Jana Prikryl

W. W. NORTON & COMPANY
Independent Publishers Since 1923

For information about permission to reproduce selections from this book, write to
Permissions, W. W. Norton & Company, Inc., 500 Fifth Avenue, New York, NY 10110

For information about special discounts for bulk purchases, please contact W. W. Norton
Special Sales at specialsales@wwnorton.com or 800-233-4830

Manufacturing by Versa Press
Design by Chris Welch
Production manager: Julia Druskin

ISBN 978-1-324-03521-3

W. W. Norton & Company, Inc., 500 Fifth Avenue, New York, N.Y. 10110
www.wwnorton.com

W. W. Norton & Company Ltd., 15 Carlisle Street, London W1D 3BS

1 2 3 4 5 6 7 8 9 0

Contents

MIDWOOD

FIRST VOICE

Went fetal as an ear on the bed and tried to feel
the dusty blue rhomboid of window being
in the vanguard of twilight every second,
hurtling, the word impressing itself
as no hurtling would on my mind
through space on the back of this
whale turning, turning, punctual
the other cheek to that star

THE PROP

Resignation and care, the words milling
the boy and I are sick in our beds
till I had to look up the first: an
annulment and then on top or beside it
love: and I the prop in the center
if I can hold them: one thing that seems
aggressive is "balance beam,"
the beam might never get to be its own
thing, a subject, a sawhorse

FENCE POST

These girls riding bareback on their palominos down the slopes
what do they know, I thought
then I saw a train that collided with a convoy
of trucks, each vehicle and each car interlocking at precisely the right moment
like gears in a fine piece of machinery
so they went through each other, the train and the convoy,
it took some time for them
to move through each other and then each went its own way

MIDWOOD 1

Out of the garment of the land
out of the
of

There in the ravine the place
that's deepest,
bent

TRAVELING PLAY

But in the night passing my apartment
you came into my bed, or was it yours
as we lay chastely side by side, a knife and spoon
your friends below had come this way
to wave up to your window then
I'd button a coat with the tags still on
to pick up some food, walk through a sudden
neighborhood, become a young woman
in a traveling play, but now did not dare move

FIRST AUBADE

Morning a telescope
have you ever had so much time
geographic folds
upon and upon and upon,
I fed an animal some grass
when Europe and America were
five inches closer to each other
its pupils were rectangular

The men have filled aubade
with pique but sun
my rival for no one
to see us turning pours out space,
I sit on the fire escape first thing
these days and organize the frames

ANOTHER VISIT

A flock of Boy Scouts dispersing early morning
from the summits down into the valley
while I looked from the window of another
visit to that city, considering the bus routes
I'd sew together along the rim of the hills
and the park tucked under the shoulder of a slope
I mean to see but never do, made of transparencies
that dropped their leaves on top of leaves
description fails, it's there without me

MIDWOOD 2

Out of the
garment of the
if you can't go
too far don't fear
how often earth
carries you, east
faster and more
gallantly

EACH LETTER

Everyone crowded in that movie theater
you found a seat to my left some thirty years later
saying little, facing the screen while I use my hair
to screen the sudden velocity of time
then you stood behind my row in that gray sweater and said
don't be hurt if I have nothing to say, I have trouble
connecting with people these days, and left only after
we folded and folded giant sheets of paper
we both had filled with alphabets
as though we would draw an animal for each letter next
and give them away to children, not what you used
to trace with a finger, slow words on my back or thigh or hand
and I on yours, a correspondence absent light or sound
especially useful around others, in a car, at the dinner table

A STORY

Home through woods having left the car behind
a man stopped to ask of me, I backed away into
the fabric store, late reopened, banter of capable women working
the front and back ends, I blinked at their nearness to all that material

AND HARDLY

And hardly had I stepped in the great limestone institute
your mother purchased with her Pulitzer
studded with Regency putti than was touring
her exhaustive collection of crotchet, like
samples piled in cubbyholes beetling a mile, surprised
you're taken in by the stacked illusion of crates
of ale, going nowhere, flat, I slowly concluded
deserving you was not my problem but by then
you were for the sake of argument installing me
in your lap so I said to myself I owed it to myself

WINDOW SEAT

Out of the fold in my mind that nearly swallowed it
the plane flew, dropping textbooks of some kind
over cities in Germany, a not entirely
benign scheme, I took a seat at the window, all the out of work
musicians grouped on street corners
playing electrified songs for almost no one
the dream pressing in as bald as the moon, no atmosphere
unstoppable that entire geography lapping you

THE PAINTER

Lucid in their maplike zones, organs, kidney, lung,
sole of the foot, unbiased as to color or tone
with luminous tint not thought today reliable
in a work of art this canvas filled by the woman painter
gave a monologue into the fisheye to thank
the reviewer for his assessment, her first
real nod, the camera angled like a mirror in a bistro
tilted downward slightly at the tables in
imitation of works of art in art palaces
she coiffed, sleeves puffed, eyebrows
rising and falling, the two verticals between
coming and going, subtracting almost nothing

MIDWOOD 3

Out of the garment
of the land—   trees and their upholstery,
tubers, among
unnamable shapes:
press your nose and the divorce unfurls,
orchid in an empty lot
not mine, the general one
a bend

THE THEATER

We browsed and as usual that one I hadn't read.
At showtime we lay down between the stacks
where we could only listen to the actors. Our faces close,
my hands tucked under my chin and legs drawn up
like an animal's. I felt such tenderness for you and knew
it wasn't returned—this as usual I couldn't understand.
Before, when our plane landed in the river
behind another that had done the same,
dunked its passengers then pulled itself up
and over to the gate with harm to none,
you weren't surprised. You had that
confidence we wouldn't sink. I couldn't understand
but both of us were walking through the gate by then,
untouched by danger. Surprise was my own possession.

AGAINST MUSIC

Wood-paneled basement like the inside of a tree for delinquent dads
held a dance class for composers, I'd walked
and now needed to get home after the cups and cups
of lemon juice used to counteract their blindness
so they'd know which way to move,
one taste, a sip
sufficient to direct them they were that sensitive, wow
yet somehow my eyes are all I need to get me where I'm going

MIDWOOD 4

Tall ones
this airport weather, an April
processing this way from which
direction I can't tell, for you is
individual, like dollars owed or
today's shirt,
you stand looking gently
down shaking heads
preparing us, your very slow branches saying little

THE SUMMIT

Into the mountains on skis, I carried
our lunch on a tray, the boy between us and you
up ahead swinging on pines
whooping, we sighing looking
up, calling lunch, when all at the top of one you came level
with a fusty bouquet deep window sill arranged
a young man who showed us around, delighted to learn
his room, two futons facing one way like a child's game of bus
made him, to us, a true bachelor

THE NONCELLO

Noncello, an ordinary river
in the north, coincidence?
the places I long for are parted by water
tension on the surface of the Noncello
even riding low, it looked like it was brimming
every ripple made of a meniscus
which, imperceptible as body
how it reached you was the tempo, stately tempo, of its flow

THE DIRT

That small woman with prematurely gray hair
hands chapped and divorced, a Yorkshire accent who worked
in the bookstore that gave me spending money fell in love
with my friend and threw herself
in the dirt for not being good enough.
Square of dirt round the bole of a tree.
But later we convinced her that she was,
she dusted herself off

OUR SECOND

A closed current
as small as a necklace
this water. Looking down at the pebble beach
from a window as tall as story. They'd done the tests
and only later I thought, nobody said
looks good. I don't mind losing the baby
our second, just interfere with the first.
But I was big and worried for myself. Pain or danger
and didn't want to see its face—I see it already—
made wrong by virus. Down there the pebble beach
our friends, comparing their finds, worried I'd solve this
the easy way, unaware one thing constantly
enters another, becoming not one with it
but taking its place, and on and on, a current

MIDWOOD 5

Out of the garment of the land
      it is not spring, why then you say
rank, but isn't
an oracle around perimeter of which
the words their lipid speeds pull from
and here so on the face of it
reserve, is it a reservoir
      if spill headfirst another's shape

LITTLE ROOM

He and I industrious on facing couches in a room
with small windows, trying to solve the problem
and he'd written four questions with sample answers
I was to amend, it was our task to formulate the lines that bring about

a way out and I saw, as I looked at the little spears of the
succulent just piercing the surface of the water I'd planted in college
I'd never have his depth or sharpness of perception and it wasn't only
that I'd never deserve him, it was how little I could gather from his questions

and extraction seemed the whole work of reading when I saw
he'd also filled the back of the page, I'd never see
with more than these few blunt cones, no way to better myself
as there was almost no way out of this room, I said I'm sorry

you're always on top and I'm on the bottom, following this
with a helpless I meant that intellectually
and felt such remorse for myself, he leaned back
against the armrest by now absorbed in something else

A LIDO

An earthquake woke the baby.
The quake that hit when I was a child
I must be sick, the nausea my own
because the region was so stable
the hero honeyed and thick with summer swimming
in a lido, his buddy joined him when our boy
refused to know him through his many
laps and tucks and dives it was so funny
I came into the morning laughing

A BANQUET

But having braked all the way to the floor of the valley
it dawned on us the slope we'd have to climb
and it was night, you on the back of my bike
we'd passed the place that burned down—the people
rich enough to continue to produce some kind
of banquet, placing candles and dishes, in the ashes
beyond roof—so you said let's go home, but look
the hill we came down is as steep as the hill ahead of us

MIDWOOD 6

The still air still through every branch
not warm, no, spring this year
a Parisian, cold and controlled
and when reserve of this variety
combines with stillness, suspends the visas
of the wind and strands the season's envoy
in another country, the quiet is
wordless but voluble, it comes right up to you to take a look

ALMA MATER

The young man grown tall and loose in every way
his clothes a drapery, reddish curling hair
a sort of cushion all around his head, providence,
was standing with a friend on campus as I pass
they're telling who accepted them for masters
intruding then I walk him there, my alma mater, scuffing
gravel on the shoulder gradually he turns female
describing in detail her plan to get pregnant
I line up my stories, not having a child
the worst thing that nearly happened to me
and it happened for years, I couldn't see the moon
in the sky without shooting dirty looks but once arrived
the boy the most arduous exacting work
I couldn't have done it alone, no please, don't try

THE NONCELLO

We found a park on the banks of the Noncello
a public park, a lawn for all, for anyone to kiss
first spotted him a night or two before
still center of a crowded bar
alone with pamphlets, advanced in middle age
went up to him, said what I can't remember
except my tone
the fool aware of his position, embracing it

THE SWIMMER

A man who does not exist, waylaid near his home
in round glasses, lean, white hair trimmed close
pauses enriching the camera operated by whom,
industrial shore—water lapping in, each wave
a brown brief saucer—how every morning he comes
and swims, an image of listeners nowhere in mind
eyes down and syntax unspooled with that air of uprightness
pertaining to intimate data held out in the hand

FIRST WIFE

The elevator swung like a boat
in its shaft on the way up. Then to grab
what clothes I could—what terrible
choices I'd made all my life with pants
I thought—and run. Part spy thriller
featuring dad's first wife who rose
to ornament beauty contests on TV, part
historical drama irised on me
racing to apply enough makeup
but the under-butler who would become
my husband was okay with this handsome
face that Jacques Maritain made famous

MIDWOOD 7

No one makes of sibilants
a thing as soft as you
do, choral motion
you
insinuate nothing, no
you tell it plain, alone
can be direct, since
so consonant with

GENTLY SPILLING

With Mary on the sofa postmortem
who driving me freeways' modern loops
where unresponsible teens wassailing not
just on curbs but spilling into
our lane gently
suggesting yes, I'd made my intentions
too obvious for
that subtle
young man, I crumpled under a blanket
on the floor, no more cushion or really
clothes to hold me in that pleasant house
storing many intelligent bodies for a lecture
I washed Fred's decanter while the whiskey
was in it, that was a mistake

ANOTHER TIME

It started another time in me
a flock of Boy Scouts dispersing early morning
from the summits down into the valley
in Rome the doctor German

when I looked from the window of another
visit to that city, silver at the temples
he used his kindest tone, considering the bus routes
I'd sew together along the rim of the hills

residing in the narrowness of its opening to regret
tucked under the shoulder of a slope
sounding almost casual, oh
I mean to see but never do, the heartbeat's gone

it's very common, he said
extracted kindness from that too
assurance a baby could one day
that dropped their leaves on top of leaves

TEN O'CLOCK

Holding perfectly still at this party
a clutch of talkers, he's at my four o'clock
you are at ten and you've cupped the fingers
of my left hand with the fingers of your left hand
as though no one will notice the little link
my whole occupation is holding still
so this may continue
all my feeling refuses
to toss the pebble in the current

CHILD STAR

Your friend the child star invited us in,
how to refuse Ben Foster
and tall ceilings, lines clean of the west?
Symmetrical, we took a room like theirs
before anyone had children
when little things still bothered me, like your time
alone with a wedding in France, and our son whom
I'm trying to get home—stalled subway, immensely
tall airplane on runway, veering shuttle bus with him
in my lap—how I miss the beach, a lithesome girl
of twenty-five who stayed up all night then slept in
and when she woke at Ben's house my envy, my envy
while the city below spreads out its map, all mine
I had the feeling I'd like to go for a walk

OTHER WORDS

When you're working the two
billows of meaning nothing
>airbags<
nudge you from either side
as you try to keep in touch with the single
wire of meaning that runs into the future
in other words the absence of meaning
also is a guide

LILAC TREES

You must have a love for that window
with busted blinds where though the glow is apricot
your angle hides the fixture on the ceiling, received
and there's the possibility of buzzing the door
the danger, that is, you might not stop yourself
embarrassing to be such an individual here
trailing these accidents
the pavement always stayed beneath my feet before

MIDWOOD 8

Out of the sheath dress
gently hopping, sparrow in the lot below
in the great complacency of summer
pressing down, waves of it
what can the plants do but endure this closeness
the trees, their varieties, and ivy, nameless shrubs
and hedges, no one speaks their names
only flowers get that nod and certain grasses
so that when a day of cooler breath in July
airs out the neighborhood you feel
for a moment the rustling in lindens, oaks, sycamores
as they sense what's been withheld
for months, that's when the mature ones
rustle it off, slip almost
sexily out of that dress, unbearable
to feel such potential against one's skin

VERTIGO ZOOM

I couldn't find my manuscript after you walked in
a soaring feeling of inadequacy
love has always been, as you addressed the room tundra and highway
through the glass behind were rising up toward your silhouette
a Vertigo zoom, I understood then this attraction
attends to your background most of all perhaps
and isn't that a shared possession
mine already, dull with use
the opposite

FIELD TRIP

And scrambling down the hill
steep as scree, soft loam under dry leaves punctuated by standing figures, trees,
I came to the rear of the school groups and followed them against my inclination
up the mountain, jogging under the chairlift
Amanda who was friendly
and unattractive in an almost fascinating way riding upward to my right
uncomfortable with her weight
There'd been those two slim women in leather jackets
getting wet teaching children how to swim
in a kiddie pool, showing me its faucets
I felt too inward, unwilling to immerse myself
though down that slope
I'd picked up a small jacket
meaning to carry it the rest of the day in case I found its owner

ANOTHER VISIT

The dark is drying up in the window
soon it will be all stain
everyone asleep my dream already clinging to the upper atmosphere
a noiseless crush the summer
I'm nineteen, Ella pouring amber *say it's only a paper* through
his bookshop, I dust the spider of postcards (how
do you dust postcards) and carry outside one at a time
a few old hunks of limestone to weigh it down

MIDWOOD 9

The same wind pushing through these leaves
turning up the palms of their hands
stop stop, who while it blows
speak their minds,
forms words foreign to us by the seashore
colder, no
words at all just demonstration of power
a flyover, depressing

THE NEED

These four ladies and I drove near
my childhood planted with dull unmythical
grass, a flat place for a getaway
to rent a cabin, trooped inside with all our bags
to find there was no key, the dream was me
appealing to a local behind the counter
who wouldn't hand over the key, magnificent
in her indifference, not asking why
we'd need a key, not stooping to debate
the need, unmoved by the variety
of my rhetorical turns, refusing to give us
the key because there was no key

THE NONCELLO

No, between the bar and the Noncello
a small table near midnight al fresco, mincing
I capered on my inner parapet and his quiet at last
perceived its advantage, leaned back
This I perceived but did not rein me in
indignity to be reined in by such a thing
it was I who had recognized him
as able to see me, diminishing myself itself a triumph

LIVING ROOM

The one to be mastered is you
yet I keep trimming the sheets around
my person with these, the little man who's four
got us up for sunrise in the living room
because it's very beautiful he said
as color toweled off, the sun
adjusting the face it wears all day,
but mama it looks like the sun is setting

FOREST GREEN

On that enormous ship peopled by our friends was one
pale, not in great shape, long dark hair, I longed for who kept going
his own way until he hung the forest green towel from his shoulders
like a cape and took the dingy out behind him with a rope
telling our friends as he pushed off what kind of superhero he was
and I swam after, he'd not object to that, around the corner
of the stern he let me kiss him so long it seems unlikely now
we couldn't touch bottom the whole time and after
convinced we'd have another
I stood adjusting my outfit forever, gray swimsuit dry
not quite reaching my nipples no matter how much I yank
under a shirt and jeans, before going back on deck to look for him

MIDWOOD 10

Nodding their pages at you
at night they turn into
the first, the earliest trees
when everything you didn't know was darkness in the woods
and now it looks
like darkness was the form
of knowledge,
you can't unsee it again

THE COACH

Players from opposing teams practiced together
sending the soccer ball up as one clear bell
after another and I whispered to an ear
beside me, do you think parity with such splendor
is possible in the other arts but the coach
heard and advised me to keep my distance
from comparison, he had the face
I now see of the squire in Bergman's film

A SAMPLE

An earthquake woke the baby
it was painful for about twenty seconds
the quake that hit when I was a child
I must be sick, the nausea my own

then the doctor pronounced me
"perfectly normal," oh really
because the region was so stable
there was another getting that shot

of dye and each had to give a sample
in a lido, the hero honeyed with summer swimming
his buddy came and when our boy refused
to know him through his many tucks and dives

I knew I'd not be satisfied
till I spied her date on the label,
that this woman is four years my elder
I came into the morning laughing

BUS ROUTES

The open air
bus careening after
our Polish driver
it could not escape,
the hills' fine creations
my phone polygraphs
humpback beauty
all set to unseat us

MIDWOOD 11

That summer when the leaves were at their fluffiest
I issued daily memos on what you mean
the leaves burned neon and suffered the brutish tassels
of the squirrels, wagging sectors of the tree with no notice
as if there were a soul inside scratching itself
it was during just that season
my task to refuse all symbols
to read you clearly, install you across from this

IT HAPPENED

My blind date arrived, our child
stored in the bedroom of my girlhood, my pants down
hair and all, at the foot of a sweeping staircase
a call about the fellowship in Sweden I bluffed
in the booth from It Happened One Night
you gashouse palooka, wood-paneled with its little
kidney-shaped table at pube level
I said I'd go, I'd be honored, but after all this had passed

OTHER FRIENDS

We roamed in air, was it a chopper or a plane,
high above the green plate of water and long tube
of waterfall, far below as a map, real as the Salzkammergut
we had the day and four enormous geese
followed into our room where my young son turned one
into a man, he held
the vicious other three and would not let them bite.
We roamed in air and scanned the water far below,
the distance itself a holiday as was his sympathy for
my fear of heights, it isn't cheating if he keeps telling me
about his wife and I enjoy the tales. The thought
of other friends as we roamed there whose marriages
were wrecked came in, were sent away, was not
a man I'd longed for or even considered much

WAITING ROOM

The solid gabled house
established in an unfortunate position
at the top of a cliff the height of a forearm
seawater incessantly nagging the front door
was the waiting room, no one makes eye contact here
each gets a pager that tells her where to go
they take some blood or poke a wand toward the ovary
ten minutes later I'm underground, appear at the office too early

DREAM HOME

The camera raking right to left, or was it left to right
across the garden seen so often in her posts, the dwelling itself discreetly
out of frame, the garden filling up bottom to top
with Queen Anne's lace, and now the camera panning sideways
allowed the front of the house, limestone blocks, that amber tone when sunset
leans on an eighteenth-century town, was almost too much for me to take in
this woman's house, who is my age
I saw why she never shared it

MIDWOOD 12

Out of the
what if what is
emerging
don't look
meanwhile the trees are doing their thing
late August thing, sounds like they need some moisturizer
sere, that tapping sound, not water
what if what is emerging is what's here

THE SIDECAR

We'd rented a house by the sea, the pictures hadn't lied
but taken maybe from a roof across the road, the house
turns out choked among houses, I took the baby
for a walk through tall grasses by the shore of all maritime history
and found the high wooden framework of men harvesting salt
the skinny beams going up and up in a college classroom
Hugh confessed his father was Lindbergh and we watched his plane
go down again, explaining everything about Hugh
I buried my face in the shoulder beside me when his mom
in the sidecar perceived he wouldn't level out, they did crash
he'd be damned if he saw those benefits go to everyone in the South
this softened the class to Hugh's baseness, because he'd also suffered

HOW KIND

How kind of you
to turn it down
to crickets, the possible is here
in every judgment I try on
against myself, if you enjoy
a more original surmise
then too I grow
acquainted with regret

HIGH TIDE

In a bustle and Victorian face, puffy and creased, who ran a girls' school
walked me round the red-brick square, that ringing tread
in front of the bookstore where she'd found me, shopgirl
her left hip pressed against my right, her left arm rigid up and down my chest

at first untoward and certain to get us thrown out
but soon was moaning, begging her to move
her body this way or that, she shushed me as she worked, done deal
I'd be accepted but when she returned her young deputy banished me

to the store while they sat in the square hashing out the list,
a surprisingly small lumpy envelope and Edwin made a remark
behind as I straightened a display of books I hadn't read that weren't selling
too late they'd installed a sea wall against the path the girls took from school

another one drowned when the tide rushed in, the headmaster weeping in close-up
as a new train rode the aqueduct a mural appeared
between the arches for the dead girl, I was there only to observe
the pupils already loaded on the cars above, roaring toward the mainland

THE NONCELLO

Sitting quietly apart, apartment man,
it was his always dwelling beside
not in and then his watchfulness
I'm picturing it now
lit by that hint of a smile
neither sweet nor cynical,
independent
also, to an extremely sharp degree, ready
Nick Arden in a chair basically

MIDWOOD 13

Out in the open trees behave differently.
They stand differently, their posture is different.
They might look at you
if that held any interest.
They really dare live alongside,
coexist. Their enormity
which doesn't need your lifted gaze
has time in it. Where we live, planted
in the span between sidewalk and street
they play their part with competence
and often commitment, invested.
They're good at being trees.

TALL TALE

I wore my yellow sundress in a little depression

the asphalt like pumice, broken in imitation of nature,

on the phone when you came by, I sensed you were about to say

Do you know how much I've loved you and I said, Oddly yes

but have been baffled as to why

and you're so great, the word expanded into meaning when it left me

the starbursts going off in my chest, our shoulders touching

and you now beside me in the little depression, where anyone might see us

EYE CONTACT

A lens on a drone hovered across the road from the glass
penthouse as two actors went in, one turned
made eye contact allowing the lens into every room
and each decision of the persons hiding there, that's how we got them
for possession of organic fibers in their garments, we threw the book
at them of the history of weaving, noting too those rectilinear
glass panels were homemade, a lean-to, children already now dismantle
not only the penthouse but the entire structure
though they are, it is true, an architect's children

PAPER MOON

A question of whether I'd stick with the plan
of suffocating my invalid wife, conceived
meticulously my friend with the shapeless trunk
and me (I was a man), I'd hold the paper mask
over mouth and nose under a poster how-to,
but at the last moment if this were a movie
I knew I'd cover my eyes through the poisoning
so brutal, now we'd have to live with her
and when I was female it was a disaster
I could not remember the words to the song
that suited my voice, It's Only a Paper Moon
I'd sing to the dentists' group, my favorite lipstick
all watery, like applying plasma, many
times I rewrote it in the dressing room

MIDWOOD 14

Out of the garment of the dirt over there

I'm looking, ready, there's no shame in transcription I wrote

in the breakup letter never sent

it depends on your definition of transcriptive

in some cultures the transgressive *is* transcriptive

but your mind was made up, stacked with the possible in genuine tones

in other words undecided

some letters more eloquent in a drawer, waiting to sprout

SECOND AUBADE

Surfacing again
my elbow shifted disclosing what happened last night
no more posturing we'd somehow agreed
to do this and though my shyness prevailed
I closed my eyes at times and at times only looked at you
information was exchanged
you were large and soft in places, as expected
which didn't put me off, your hand offered
when I'd take nothing else, undimmed by my sudden
pulling back, quite cold in your refusal
to feel bad about this, serious about getting to the bottom of it
and at last I think if I remember correctly I could find no
argument against your seriousness, it matched
my distance from you too exactly

THE RUINS

Unprepossessing girl in the café recognized me as the author of two books
before this and asked for my advice, I said
each line has been an accident, staring at the texture
of the plaster on the wall behind her, rivulets cords tendons the lines may stand
if I remove myself, my will ruins it I might not have said that and
recalling exactly what I said would help, I wait for it though waiting
can be a mistake that generates willfulness, I struggled to put this into words
as strong as my conviction, so what advice could I give you I said

NEXT CYCLE

Holding perfectly still at this party
a blizzard begins the night before
a clutch of talkers, he's at my four o'clock
our flight home from Christmas and that day

you are at ten, you've cupped the fingers
of my left hand with the fingers of your
but first we need to reach a clinic hours away
the four of us at five a.m. like a nuclear family shouldering into the car

my old father plows through drifts on the highway
my whole occupation is holding still
hours to make the next cycle, nobody keener

to toss the pebble in the current
true love and also something else, cracked manly honor
deserves some credit for this baby science and money did nothing to produce

ON DESIRE

Why, Venus, answer
the sculptor's prayer, the bit
he couldn't bear to say out loud
you might have eavesdropped on desire
before but this
the helpless way
it's mixed with shame
seduces
have mercy, if mercy will empty you like an appetite

MIDWOOD 15

Look how lively they grow in October
wind pirouettes the leaves
the leaves still green, they revel in the dip in temperature
they think it means the next few months will be pleasanter

SECOND ATTACK

Hardly space to talk in that record shop
but after the second attack in Manhattan I stole back
not sure if you just worked there, a skinny middle age
avid way of questioning that led to real
conversation, sandy blond genial fictional man
let pass my terror of a third attack
after our side's lawless retaliation, and were kind
to my boy, came upstairs to our tiny plywood flat
shared with another mom and her daughter
sat me in a corner to mock my careless way with the doctor
whose attention I needed and our parley
reached such a wry crescendo I couldn't see
how to decline tomorrow
though by then I saw certain flaws or maybe
limitations, glancing down each foot has three toes
why are they bare, why not let it go

ANOTHER VISIT

My hair was long again
in a banana clip
yet I hoped
to be loved and
admired with this ficus
on the back of my head
walking through a city
dotted with Irish pubs

CUSTODY HEARING

Mom and I whispering, huddled on a set of bleachers that run all the way around
a conference table, behind the Czech supermodel who's gained custody
of my son because she is his mother, until I thought
no, the deep window sill in the delivery room like an airport's
I remember, and pondering an epidural with the paralysis menus instill
and when the anesthesiologist appeared with his little bucket-like tray forcing
myself to say Actually, his eyebrows going up and my goggled obstetrician telling him
She said no, then the boy squirted out so I thought, well
I cheated and she, his wife, has my baby, it's natural

THE NONCELLO

Apartment man accompanied me
the rest of that week on the Noncello
ten years ago, a child
thirty-five, a teen
Apartment man was German if you want to know
what came between us, it wasn't
the distance, it was the provenance
I couldn't do that to my dead Babi

MIDWOOD 16

Roots may want a gentle shower
the leaves are out for something else
they cannot look away
each drop a slap in the face

THE CONNECTION

You, blond, a backstop behind me in line

at the deli where the Japanese woman, her fingertips

twigs, harried, named the three kinds

of gefilte fish, none very convincing but I went

for so-called salmon while you went on

about those people, Mideasterners, their demerits you felt

I wasn't seeing a camera like a tilted cheval

on us and I remember my only possible reply

was turning the back of my head

to its silver trembling element

and then I was running for the train to Berlin

failing to make the connection eight times within

the one miss because you relive that kind of trouble

in motion and as this late interview shows

even had I been kinder to my first rush of love

for you it would've come to nothing, our destination

VAST WATERCOLORS

The house of my dreams
mainly a looping driveway, white gravel
this side of a hill, beyond which a sea
you'd bought me, huge white brick dwelling
modest for its neighborhood
the kind of thing you possess and long for simultaneously
came furnished, hung with vast watercolors
of Seventies chanteuses, their loose manes and thin limbs
mainly their stories, all that striving for something minor

MY TYPE

The silent treatment from him again today but I was sitting
on a hillside near Harvard last night, waiting for my date
and there you sat, a few groups away
a crowded slope and mainly thinking your body
is far from my type while wishing you'd come over
so I could touch you, when with a laugh you're telling that guy
his bullet-proof vest left much to be desired, take yours off
and hand it to him, take his and put it on

MIDWOOD 17

Out of the ravine I look out over
fenced off
green with a windless October
silent swims
a helium balloon, HAPPY BIRTHDAY, dented square half
deflated the other half sends up
and up, cannot express how silent its rowing, then twists
a few times and drifts over the lid of the next building, gone
now who is down there

GAME SHOW

A few of the public hushed "Armstrong hair!" to see you
Voyta, in that Hollywood Square
dangling your head like an egg over the parapet
to size up your waitress, death bestows such flexibility
then fled down the aisle, some of the zeroes in the seats
mocking your elevating soles, I too surprised you feel
you need them but busy taking down dad's apology
on a ziploc fat with ink-blue wool
what he'd say to make it visible beyond me
while you help me sneak into the building I feel
I need access to, we're all stealth on the imperial
carpet up the stairs littered with broken objects
and almost caught by those impostors
I have no reason to be here aside from your protection

A PALINODE

What is the moon
but a palinode,
going out on a limb
to say everything and then
walking it back
walking it
walking, what's that
but a way of saying it again

STAY CLOSE

Maroon and pneumatized, I'm one of those
huge men streaming through a border manned by kind
guys who enjoy classical music, one of these asks
Did you spend too long in the sun
can't disagree, muscle shirt in hand, sheepish
to be in that body but one of many in that body,
we were streaming back into the country after or before
my only thought to stay close to bodies like mine
even the dream would only let men in

THE RUNAWAY

Our heads together at that audio cassette bar
the barkeep fixing one of your old tapes
and you telling me how stressed you are
handing out a weekly fiction prize

when I said you know it's funny
a piece of writing that you can't put down
reading in a book won't keep you
if it's hung on a wall, the text has to be bound

so you can take it to a mountaintop
and incidentally this whole time
the child I'd found curled around the bole of a pine
I hadn't reported her and night was here

her parents in Ohio desperate, my fault
if she doesn't make it on that freezing height
but how to reach the oldies call-in show
at this hour they'd be flooded with requests

MIDWOOD 18

A day so overcast

the sparrows the toy ambassadors of nature

are staying in their crofts their secret hideaways

the ravine is quiet the maples with their male-pattern baldness

fluttering blond leaves at midlevel, naked candelabras on top

where are the sparrows my morning confidants

what does this shadowless lighting this dusky overture tell them

the line of every twig every fire escape achieves prominence

those letters you sent me in childhood folded in a box a whole day's drive away

ANOTHER VISIT

Walked slowly up the moraine over the sea
with our friends and separately also drove there
nearly missing the turn, at the top
a series of bungalows shaped like train cars maintained
by a branch of the government and ours
all wood and leather inside, all brown,
the bathroom a small booth that doubled as shower,
outside on the sward Pat stood with his heels
to the edge and pointed back at fires below, we smiled
to recognize our star among the refineries

HOME MOVIE

Strewn across the floors their toys and things, a video cassette the dad
had written "We used to have more of these" on,
the kitchen in a state of high party, boxed cakes half eaten, cannoli
and rows and rows of drinks were pastries brimming with cream
along the broken ramparts of the countertops, we noticed blue carpet
but hardwood elsewhere, no choice had been right
the house abandoned in haste if in triumph or terror, just
abandoned, a family photo on the wall when the twins were babies
dad diminutive and round, pale as batter, mom had great bones and a vanity
he subsidized while the babies grew through that disorder into us
and as we toured the house accepting slowly even this we can't afford
I'd love to steal the plants but how to get them home
the towering ficus and an actual tree I can't name and others
they lived at least on a larger scale, they reached for things, these half-wits

WINDY DAY

Days the wind's an animal I picture it
elsewhere, Munich or Split, inciting to riot
the spoon on the edge of the saucer
in the square, the couple there trying
to wrap it up, even the local caryatids
who've seen a few things
appear to put themselves out
that's what travel is
each part straining its hawser

MIDWOOD 19

The problem feels almost spatial this morning

beyond the maples to my left someone blasting a classics station

whose lyrics drifting here, each line I anticipate, sound tiny, tin homunculus

flawless in his proportions, in front the ordinary birds, squirrels haplessly rehearsing

to my right the ding-dong of Q train doors two blocks away, elevated

perfectly authentic but faint and then the ripples I provide

for a leaf sailing to earth, if I could tune this to the right degree

make contact—but by "spatial" I meant here with you on the page

A PROCEDURE

I had some minor surgery on Monday
yet I keep trimming the sheets around
my person with these, they put me to sleep for this
enterprising eel, eye-first, home movie

the little man who's four
got us up for sunrise in the living room
because it's very beautiful he said
it showed nothing no

explanation except my years, having assigned the blame
the doctors feel we may begin
as color toweled off, the sun
adjusting the face it wears all day,

we start right after Christmas then
and then with drugs each night
but mama it looks like the sun
to sleep I count three things that weren't completely intolerable that day

TRAVELING PLAY

Chastely in a bed side by side, knife and spoon, you confide
the piece of writing you're failing to write
on a man who adapted his movie into a play
the others were not in the room, their absence delicious
for once I could tell your idea of me was changing
in due time you might have to take my mind seriously
delightful, that feeling of anticipation, transformed
at no cost to me, but what is veiled by this moviegoing
is not my longing for you to know everything true

SOME PINES

Serried, green as paint, rising up a steep incline
above my childhood, a sort of extra forehead there
behind the house, I look back
the pines stand for my good fortune
growing up in that spot, where they were not
deciduous and the slope shot down
under them, many conversations with those trees
with leaves on and without their leaves absorbed a lot

MIDWOOD 20

It finally happened, I fell asleep puzzling
what if I'd been true, really thought of you
and fetched up on the lawn of childhood, my own turf
there a tree capered toward me as a person, a sapling

was a youth in the orange trousers of fall foliage
she scampered up the side of a mature oak
looking for the silt inside of clam shells
she'd stored in the eaves for her supper, I was too slow

to get a decent picture of her
or do more than watch from the patio
but it seemed a benevolent gesture on the part of the trees
to hint that this is what they are, like me

annoying strivers
in constant danger of making bad choices
under cover of an impishness that can't be enlarged,
examined closely, it is too close, did I think that would let me off

THE NONCELLO

Apartment man flew to America
I ran home from work, maybe freshened up at home
before running to the bar where he was parked
his suitcase stashed in back or hard by the plate glass in front
it must have been November, early dark
we sat in a booth exchanging information
gazing madly and the waitress came, he looked up
aimed that same infiltrating gaze at her, not a few lines
of dialogue testing the border
I'm amazed, silently
it is because he's European
he stayed with me his whole stay but it was over

SMALL PARTS

Somewhere between silversmith and potter

he demonstrated how he works, with his wheel

pulling the material in and shaving it away into a hole in the center

what he's making, utensils, small parts, hard to say

when Drusilla, pale from a costume drama, sashays over

to have sex in the middle of the party, her form an hourglass

her torso like the molded piece of fiberglass

I wore as I filled out to sway my scoliosis

on top of me which I can do no more than caress, cannot get in among the sands

ANOTHER VISIT

Appointed to a T-intersection at the shoulder
of town whose northeast slope
leads to Roman fortifications still sand-paved
and San Francisco steep, the sunlight filling in
uncertainties of form, the shoulder I mean to reach
but never do, arched doorways not so much into dwellings as bestride
the street, ushering a visitor from then to then
with a bow, like history, a form of art
useless gesture containing the germ of my wish

TRUNDLE BED

Where exactly was I
the black branches sway in their yellow element
behind aquarium glass, November gale, where was I
the man a bearded conglomerate
had me trapped in his top-floor apartment
I slept on a trundle bed, the rock of Victoriana, beside him
except for when he sought my body's comforts
and joined me on my level
then I resisted as far as was prudent, past that I felt nothing

MIDWOOD 21

Qua quatrain, it barreled through the night
another morning disembarks
trees look at one another, well then
the light is not egregious, it stands back to let you think
but into that clearing you hardly dare step
what is there to think about
the man whose job it is carries our garbage away

THE SPEED

The snow gave a lift careening by this yellow bus
but when we reached the stile, caesura between two freeways
installed by who knows who
upholstered in dirt—earth's tendons popping—the rain had been
too recent, sat on the bus waiting for the mud to harden
while men laid planks over it I caught my reflection in the window
and up through the windshield stepped our driver (end of her shift)
in green pantyhose (thick legs, no elegance, all power) who'd gone so fast
my heart flipped, I gained a piece of knowledge then, it hates to be in cars
the speed's not honest, the face in the glass not mine
but softened, melted over angles my face lacks, it was I see
the face Milena Jesenská possessed in her middle years, which were her last

THE STEREOSCOPE

Meticulously done and meaningless
your student had drawn a stereoscopic view of a palace
in colors complementary, intelligent
and you writhed on the bed in disappointment
a double-wide, my place near the seam, the other
couple passing through from Germany alarmed
by our drama, I was trying to comfort you doing my best
to make contact chastely along your bare legs and arms
with my bare legs and arms, that line of contact
an image of depth brought into focus

WHY NOT

The snow sparkled,
each shift
in my sled's
position
caused it to sparkle again
as I sped down that way and thought
why not
enjoy this, meaning
look at it,
so I looked, what allowance, and later

can't sleep
came back out
glance up
the sky full of unexpected stars
surprised
it looks like a vast piece
of quartz, sparkling, veiny and I thought, oh
the sky has always been like this
a rock
of course

A STORY

Old woman and man climb side by side they know
one final time escarpment cracked in two
halfway up she goes on, he lingers
at the top she gets into position
her side of a double-wide mimeo of the
bathtub of rock I found years ago on a scramble up a vast gray
forehead in Yosemite, laid myself down
where no more of the park could be seen
only sky, supine there as long as I dared
so she lay prone, head overboard, so observed
him turn away from the slope that led to her
and leap to his conclusion in salt water

MIDWOOD 22

One thing I'll say about trees
they never object
to getting carried away
I don't mean uprooted, I mean swept
sideways while also forth toward a certain place in the sky
the sun may know about
what does the sun know
I don't mean the constant burning, rather
unfortunate position, no surrender

PURPLE ROOM

You dwelled in an apartment at the top of an office building
in a society cluttered, a sailboat flying, landing become a bicycle
ran into you on the street and we caught up in bed just joking
your bedroom in the back, hung with sackcloth, tentlike attic ceiling
whole place large and lucky, as if you'd found
the better situation, the only one I felt this way about
and by the time I heard you'd died it felt remote
a slow waltz with an octopus who liked me

THE NONCELLO

Apartment man gave me some advice,

argue with him

I met the ex behind a plate glass window

when he flew home from America

at Bocca Lupo, head in his hands

for hours, felt strangely removed, for a minute

really felt I could take it or leave it

Reader, I did

well that's one way to keep you there behind the glass

JET LAG

Through the airport corridor you escort my case
there's something like a hotel room upstairs for us
before my flight out of Rome, every structure
in this city a skin tone, it's hard to take in
that I'm leaving alone, same blank feeling as when
everyone goes out and you are left at home, look at this
bizarre custom of sacrificing sleep to get anywhere
just how am I supposed to function when I get there

MIDWOOD 23

Can you reach abstraction without going through chaos
winter asked itself, replied
yes, fall was orderly
in coming apart and I learned a lot
listening fully formed inside its head
not only can you take what you want
or even what you don't particularly
but also say it, you can say anything
no place for hesitation in a realm of fog

ART DECO

The line at the store being too long
he flew, vertical, as in an elevator shaft, to a ledge
up the side of a skyscraper, I clutched his arm
there we waited like cormorants for the line to subside
he was able to will his way across the air
just thinking it translated him there
and I sat, grubbing the pebbles around my ankles as he was doing
what folly for me to leap alone once the line was short enough
how could I possibly know if my body would stay aloft

A HAIRCUT

What I said I'd do
knowing you knew what I'd wanted to
as we stood among the loose cross-hatchings
of my cut hair, the filaments, was
sweep it up, I even grabbed a broom
though in the glass you must have seen
how far I'd almost gone
and in that sense
I saw, in the reflection
a fictional broom, school janitor's wide mustache on linoleum
a villain, I'd no intention
you must have seen
of tidying my stuff
the truth was out, patternless on the tile

NEW APARTMENTS

They converted the brutalist hospital
into apartments carted up the hill
to the village where I was raised
tidy boxlike houses up till then
perplexing to see the poor living among us now
It was winter in the field behind the apartments
the field all white, pathways coated in a thickness of ice
the ice as clear as glass, or clearer, when I looked
the property of the ice that kept me from touching the gravel
forced me to see each pebble entirely as it was

MIDWOOD 24

Imperfectly descry
through fretwork goes the one
late leaf in swoon
without any trouble through
the fretting of the tree imperfectly
descry, monochrome
pattern on the eyelids as you drift to
that's the future, bud
experience
thanks to poems, plays you don't live to
what you have's an
of the tree a leaf floats through and rarely
down, the leaf, whom I have been
flies up in a swoon

MY PAPERS

Feeding coins into the copy machine at de Gaulle
it spits out the papers I need to fly home
but stopped midway
the long line of people behind me gone
when I look up, they'd found their own
dimes I hadn't failed to pack
machine won't talk, no help
when I told this one you said wow, Paris, xerox,
change, the writers have really stopped caring

HER BALLOON

Each of us gripped one side of the plank
seated as on a see-saw
making one face card high in the air
but she seemed at ease, it was her
balloon despite the total absence of lines
linking it to the hot air taking us down
off the alp, a favor on my holiday
my holiday made of wishing I lived there
with such conveyance of my own
but she let me steer and thinking alone
seemed to keep us from bumping the treetops
when we got down to our mutual friend's
I thanked her, like that
finished going over the mountain

SECOND NOCTURNAL

The glass bowl the moon makes of the sky
held off, someone was sorting cutlery below

leaves shushed, here and there traffic sobbed
yet it was as though the ocean, five miles away, had come over
as good as if waves rushed in under this fire escape
What would I do then?
I'd have it all, at the edge of the element we share
I'd have no more of wanting

Acknowledgments

Some of these poems were first published in *The American Poetry Review, The Atlantic, Granta, Harper's Magazine, The Nation, The New Yorker, The New York Times Magazine, The Paris Review, Raritan, The Times Literary Supplement,* and *The Walrus.*

A fellowship from the Guggenheim Foundation helped support the writing of this book.